100 Things Project Managers Should Do Before They Die

The following people made major contributions to the content of this book:
Dale Beyer
Mary Lofsness
Jeff Nielsen
Jess Snively

100 Things Project Managers Should Do Before They Die

100 Things
Project Managers
Should Do Before
They Die

By Rita Mulcahy

I dedicate this book to the hundreds of thousands of project managers whom I have helped apply project management to the real world. Adding a little humor makes the journey so much more FUN!

Printed in the United States of America

ISBN 13: 978-1-932735-12-3
ISBN 10: 1-932735-12-7

Library of Congress Control Number: 2008923765

RMC Publications, Inc.
Phone: 952.846.4484
Fax: 952.846.4844
E-mail: info@rmcproject.com
Web: www.rmcproject.com

Table of Contents

* The page numbers are the "tip" number.

Introduction

With all the craziness that projects can entail, sometimes we forget to have fun! Did it ever cross your mind to do something a little wacky? Between creating schedules and holding meetings, make time to enjoy the experiences suggested in this very different kind of to-do list. Take a moment to see the humor in projects again.

How to use this book

Though I would love to see you read every page of this book, you will most likely just flip through it. Keep the book with you for awhile and see how it makes you laugh and helps you generate new ideas that, surprisingly, you can use in the real world. Bring it to team meetings and share copies with your team and your sponsor.

As you read, you might think of things you would have included in this book. E-mail your ideas to 100Things@rmcproject.com and we might include them with your name in the next edition of this book.

All the best,
Rita Mulcahy

Chapter 1

Getting Your
Point Across

Answer a
question
with a
question.

Answering a question with a question such as, "Can you explain why this is important?" will help you better understand the situation before you respond.

Make the second sentence of your e-mails **gibberish** to see who is reading them.

2

I went under the sunshine to get to the moon. See, it isn't hard to write even nice-sounding gibberish. If you are sending e-mails that no one reads, why are you sending them?

Be a
crash test
dummy.

Feel the impacts of project failures as if they were physically affecting you. This will inspire you to do something to make a change. How about bringing a crash test dummy (the kind used in car safety testing) to your team meetings? At each meeting, discuss the new bumps and bruises the dummy has acquired during your project.

Include a
visit from
Superman.

4

Every project manager could use help from someone with clout. Ask the team, "If we could get Superman to help us with this project, what would we ask him to do?" This usually results in some enlightening ideas about who the bad guys are and where the project or the team really needs extra help.

Don't **talk**
for a day.

Not talking for a day will help you focus on what you really need to say and how well other forms of communication work or do not work.

Cancel
a **meeting**
and see if you
really needed
it in the first place.

6

This is a trick from one of the best project managers I know. To see whether you are using meetings effectively, cancel one of your meetings! Can you find a more effective way to accomplish what you had planned for that meeting?

Liven up
meetings.

7

If you are attending someone else's meeting and they are not following proper meeting rules, entertain yourself with any of the following diversions:

- Play table hockey with a wad of crushed paper
- Turn off the lights and use cell phones as flashlights
- Organize swivel-chair Olympics

Experience
the value of
nonverbal
communications.

8

Have you ever noticed that much of what is communicated to you is not what is said, but how it is said and the body movements used to express it? Start paying attention, and see how much more you learn.

Serve
espresso
to speed up
meetings.

9

Make your meetings more productive and more fun. No one likes to waste time in long, drawn-out meetings.

Ask
5 to 10
questions
about why
the project is
being done.

10

Many project managers take the information about a project and just start working. Better project managers make sure they understand all the "whys" of the project to help them make better decisions throughout the life of the project.

Hold a team meeting on the **Great Wall of China.**

Okay, how about somewhere other than where your meetings are usually held?

Changing people's regular environment often opens them up. It shows that you are an excellent project manager who cares about your team. Having a meeting in an interesting location, even if it is just a fun local restaurant, will energize your team members and increase productivity and cooperation. But make sure you follow proper meeting rules, even out of the office.

Include project **party pictures** in project reports.

There is a secret behind this idea: You will show that your projects are fun. When word gets around, you will have more cooperation on your existing project and more people will want to work for you in the future.

Don't
e-mail
for a day.

It seems so easy to just send a message when you are at your computer, but relying on this form of communication can make you lazy. Perhaps it is time to get out of your chair, get to know your team members personally, and walk around your office to really see what is going on.

Chapter 2

Minding the
Details

Determine the **benefit cost ratios** for all decisions.

When you look at the cost of each benefit, you might start to realize how much work is being done that is not worth the investment of time and cost.

Spend
time with the
procurement
department.

The procurement process includes creating the contract, which consists of the scope of work, the number of meetings, and the types of reports the project requires. Aren't these tasks that you would normally be involved in on a project? A contract should never be signed without your input. Make this happen by getting to know the procurement department.

Build a house of **dominoes** with your team or supplier.

This is a fun activity to demonstrate how one glitch can affect the entire project.

Assume everyone is your **friend.**

Why not? Have you noticed how far those who do this advance in companies? People who are not your friends are just not your friends YET.

Manage **cost** on the project even though management does not have a cost budget.

What exactly is the benefit of managing cost? Is it ethical to spend more than necessary to complete a project? Could an actual cost that exceeds the estimate indicate that too much work is being done, and an actual cost that is significantly lower than the estimate indicate that the product is being produced with poor quality? Measuring cost helps you know if the risk, quality, schedule, and other components of the project are in line with the project plan.

Make your
boss sign a
contract
with you.

19

The position of "boss" has roles and responsibilities. Just as you owe your boss your work, loyalty, and support, your boss owes you similar consideration. Why not include these in a contract? This will make both of you realize your respective obligations.

Put crime scene tape around a **poorly performing** project.

20

It is not always the project manager's fault when a project is in trouble. Maybe you need more support or attention from senior management. Certainly, you can issue a report saying you're over budget or behind schedule and the reasons for it, but that might not draw anyone's attention. Putting crime scene tape around your project is sure to get management's attention.

Bring your boss an
apple.

In many parts of the world, students bring their teachers an apple as a token of appreciation. Isn't your boss a teacher? What would happen if you brought an apple to your boss and said, "Thank you, teacher"? Might your boss realize the role he or she plays in your career? This is a great trick to use whether you have a good or bad relationship with your boss. Watch how your boss's attitude changes.

Make
friends with a
contractor.

22

You could also befriend a buyer or a client. Many project managers often get caught up with the problems that sellers or buyers may cause. It is easy to forget the other party's perspective. Through making friends with a seller (if you are a buyer), you will be able to understand his or her point of view and you will be better able to work with sellers on projects in general. How much do you think that would help you?

Create a budget
thermometer.

Use a poster of a thermometer to illustrate advancement toward project completion. Display it for everyone to be able to see your project's progress.

Have a **party** when a risk occurs to **celebrate** that you were prepared.

Read this one again. It means that you and your team members are happy and excited when a problem occurs. How different is this from your real world? How good would it feel to say, "We have a plan for that!"? Is this real world? Well, not really. Using your team members' and your experience, I bet you can come up with a list of almost all the things that could go wrong on your project.

Actually meet your
budget.

25

Manage project cost as if it were coming out of your own pocket.

Identify all the **sharks** lurking beneath the surface of a project.

26

Sharks bite, and there might also be risks that can bite you on your project. Yet, many people are mistakenly afraid to talk about things that can go wrong on their projects, as if not acknowledging the issues will make them go away. Some project managers wait for a problem to occur and then act like they are saving the day when they fix it. In reality, finding and preventing (or planning for) problems before they happen saves cost and time on the project. A great way to look for these things without seeming too negative is to ask team members, "What might bite you on this project?"

Sponsor
your own project.

You complain and complain about project sponsors, but what would you do if you were in their shoes? Would you do the same thing? Walk a mile in your sponsor's shoes, and you will see why it is not so easy to be a good sponsor.

Say **"no"**
to just one thing.

Although project managers try to meet all the
stakeholders' needs, it is not always possible.
Sometimes you need the courage to say "no"
and mean it!

Ask everyone who provides you an **estimate,** "What will happen if your estimate is wrong?"

Will they think of the impact to themselves?
Will they think of how a poor estimate might
hurt the project or the company? Do they
really know the consequences?

Be the one to **shorten** the schedule.

Management does this to us all the time, but why should management (or the customer) have all the fun? Why not be the one to find a new way to shorten the project time and still meet the customer's needs? Come on, you have lots of experience! Can't you find a way?

Create
opportunities
on your project
that did not
exist before.

31

An opportunity is an event that affects your project in a positive way. For example, you could:

- Get your project noted in the local newspaper. This will generate good publicity for your company and help you gain more business.
- Turn an expense into a profit by reselling your new-found expertise or by reusing an aspect of your project.

Looking for opportunities adds more value to the project.

Chapter 3

Shaping Your
Success

Play the song **"We're Not Gonna Take It"** every time someone asks for a scope change.

32

Are you still laughing about this one? I am, even though I am reading it for the fifth time. Why not find a fun way to deliver the message that changes are not always a good thing? Remember, too many changes means that you have not managed the project well.

Try to write and arrange **music** or choreograph a **dance.**

33

After all, a project manager is like an orchestra leader. On a project there are frequently people who are experts in their fields, just as in an orchestra there are people who are expert musicians. The experts know what they need to do. An orchestra leader doesn't tell someone how to play the violin; he or she helps orchestrate all the parts into a cohesive whole. Becoming more familiar with art forms like music and choreography will remind you of what you are trying to do as a project manager.

Plan to take a
ridiculous
vacation.

34

You use project management every day, but do you ever use it for your benefit outside of work? Not only would that help make your nonwork-related projects better and faster, but it would also allow you to try new project management applications or aspects of project management that you don't normally use in your work. Try using project management to plan a ridiculous vacation, such as visiting the largest roadside attractions in the United States.

Spend a week
not touching
software.

35

"What?" you might ask, "Is this possible?" Of course it is. The question to ask yourself is, "Should project management focus on using software?" It is easy to get caught up in software while neglecting the primary functions of project management, which are managing people and preventing problems.

Lead a **tour**
of your project.

This one makes you think, doesn't it? Does your project look like a messy home that you wouldn't dare let guests visit? Think of the part of your project you would show to someone who came for a tour, and make it sparkle.

Make a
dartboard
out of your WBS.

At each team meeting, take turns throwing darts at your WBS to remind the team of your project's target.

Plan a project as if you **owned** what you were building or creating.

Would you want everything to be perfect?
Would you ask more questions and encourage
the team more than you currently do? Would
you be a little more concerned about the cost,
schedule, and impacts to your life as the project
was completed? Why don't you do that for the
rest of your projects?

Watch
an inspiring
movie
and draw project
management tips
from it.

Consider watching *The Miracle Worker*, *Apollo 13*, or *Field of Dreams*. When you start to see project management everywhere, you will realize all the ways it can be used.

Shoot a
**gold
plater.**

A gold plater is someone who expands project scope by adding functionality or other work that is not called for in the project plan. Some project managers I know have signs on their desks reading, "Gold platers will be shot!" Others keep soft, spongy "bullets" at team meetings to "shoot" gold platers.

Why is gold plating so bad? The extra work might not be needed or valued. Imagine that someone came to clean your house and saved all the dirt from your floor in a special jar he or she ordered, and then sealed the jar and labeled it with your name and the date. Would you appreciate this gold plating? Would you like to pay for the time and cost of filling the jar?

Use your five
senses
in project
management.

41

You might never have asked yourself, "How does my project smell?" but if your project smells, you certainly have a problem. How about asking yourself if there is something you are not hearing in an important conversation? What are you not seeing when you have an important problem to solve? To discover the real issues the project is facing, ask your team members, "What do you want to change on this project so badly that you can taste it?"

Measure
the **quality** of
your own project
management
performance.

42

You track project performance and evaluate others, so why not measure your own abilities as a project manager? How did you do in creating the project communication plan? Why not take out a project management book and compare your plan with what is suggested, and then rate yourself? How did you do with risk management? Did you act as a mentor for your team? How about keeping conflict under control? Create metrics in these or other areas of your own performance. Remember that the better you do, the easier your projects will be and the more success you will experience. Isn't it worth it?

Create a
**lessons
learned**
for improving
your own project
management.

43

Stop right now. Do you ever stop and just think? Lessons learned are immensely valuable to the team and to the company. They document what was done right, what was done wrong, and what would be done differently if a project (or a part of a project) could be redone. Lessons learned can help the team and everyone involved on your project. In addition, lessons learned serve as a resource for future teams that might refer to your project records for information or ideas. What about applying this to yourself? Have you ever written down lessons you have learned so that you can use them in the future?

Create a
network;
be a
network.

44

Do you have a network of people with whom you can share information? Why not? This is one of the 15 attributes of the best project managers, and something you can easily start to do. A network allows you to gain and provide support, advice, information, and knowledge.

Figure out
how you will
do all aspects of
**project
management**
before you do the
actual work.

45

A project manager's main focus should be to plan how the project will be managed and then to manage it. The focus is not to deal with problems. Why not try this out on your next project?

Do a project **outside** your field.

46

Project managers should be able to manage any type of project, because project managers bring project management skills to the project rather than technical skills. Why not test this? Try something new. It will help kick-start your career and will give you a chance to apply project management tools from another perspective.

Call attention
to your project
charter.

Has your project ever gotten off track? Has anyone forgotten what your project is trying to accomplish? This won't happen again if you make your project charter into a curtain and hang it over the entrance to your meeting room as a reminder of your mission. Or use your charter as a computer screensaver. Putting your charter on everyone's desktop keeps it visible. Your team members will be more likely to keep the goal in mind while working on your project.

See a shuttle
launch.

48

Think of all the project management that goes into a shuttle launch. Then think of the project management that went into the car you ride in or the building you work in. Realize that good project management makes a difference, not only in outer space, but in the real world as well.

Take more **preventive** actions than **corrective** actions.

How good would you feel if you completed a project without having to fix anything? Do you spend too much time fixing problems now? Why? Have you ever thought it might be because you did not properly plan the project?

Reinvent
history.

If only they had you in the past. What would you have been able to accomplish? For example, "When the Egyptians built the pyramids, they could have saved resources by doing _____."

Try to
manage a
project without a
WBS.

What? You are not using one now? My, how much time you have been wasting on your projects! If you have not used a WBS, now is the time to start. If you use one now, stop and see just how much more difficult your project becomes without one.

Come up with **silly names** for all your past projects.

52

If you could rename all your past projects, what would you name them? Do you see any trends in the names you come up with? If your projects could be called "The Joker," "The Green Monster," "The Change Makers," or any similar name, realize that these are your projects. You should have been in charge, so such names could apply to you.

Create a **WBS** for a project you've already finished.

This is a great way to see how much more efficient the project could have been if you had organized and broken it down differently. There are no good or bad WBSs, only better ones.

Chapter 4

Leading with a New Perspective

Celebrate a **holiday** from a **culture** other than your own.

Projects can be full of issues and challenges when different cultures are involved. Make cultural differences interesting. Allow them to broaden your horizons.

Write a short
story of your
successes
that will inspire
others to use projec
management.

Why not share good news? The successes you
and your team have achieved could encourage
others. Don't you feel you have had success
others could benefit from?

Volunteer to teach project management to a **nonprofit** organization.

Many people who work in organizations that are not designed to make a profit are superb at what they do, but they often have little business training. A skilled project manager like you could help them make the most of their efforts. They need you!

Share **stories** from each team member's home country.

57

Hearing a story of how someone gave up months of work time to participate in the Carnival in Rio de Janeiro is fascinating. Such stories make the world seem smaller and more interesting, and make each team member feel part of the team.

Read
a book on
the part of project
management
you least like.

Is it communications or detailed scheduling that you really do not like or are uncomfortable with? Reading a book on the topic will help you open your eyes to some of its benefits, or you will at least be better able to stomach it.

Taste
warrior life.

If you're familiar with RMC Project Management, Inc., you'll notice we often use the image of a sword on our course materials. As a project manager, aren't you a warrior? You're protecting something that's important. You're out there making sure that everything that needs to be done is done. So why not act more like a warrior than you normally do? Why not fight for your cause, instead of being rolled over? Just imagine that you're an ancient warrior you've read about in history books: maybe you're a Trojan warrior, a Viking, or a conquistador. Why can't you be like that person in your project management work? What would be different if you were?

Do something worth **broadcasting.**

Projects can help make a difference in the world. Have you ever thought about it that way? If you help make a difference, why not do something worth getting on TV or radio?

Learn something
that only a
native
would know
about a team
member's
country.

The world is full of interesting things. Did you know that in the New York City area in the United States, there is an expression called "GU," meaning someone who is "geographically undesirable"? It is used to refer to someone you meet but cannot be friends with because he or she lives too far away. Some people you meet in New York City live two hours away from the city. I know you will remember that story. When you see me, tell me you remember it and I will laugh because I'll know that at least one person is reading what I write. Do you think such stories might be an easy way for team members to get to know one another? How might that help communication and prevent some conflicts?

Say,

"Yes, but…"

more often.

62

A good project manager will always say, "Yes, but…" Can you say, "Yes, but…"? When you say that, you imply that you can do anything; you can get the project done in half the time, you can get the project done at half the cost, etc.; however, something has to change. The "yes, but…" is backed up with detailed research about the tradeoffs. Do you have that strength? If not, why not?

Learn all the ways
"project"
is spoken or written
throughout the
world.

Just think of how interesting you will be at work parties.

Be known for being **generous** with your time and help.

Why not start this one NOW?

Invent a **word** that makes it into project management nomenclature.

Maybe "supercalifragilisticexpialidocious" is not the best choice, but I think you get the idea.

Work **virtually** with people from another country.

You do this already? Good! As you are reading this book, are you realizing that you have already done some of the things we suggest you do before you die?

Be a project
hero.

A hero displays courage and self-sacrifice in the face of danger and adversity. Does this describe you, or are you always putting yourself first? How could you be a hero to your team, sponsor, client, or even to another project manager?

Chapter 5

Creating
Teamwork

Spend a
day working
from your
intuition.

68

Intuition is the ability to sense or know something immediately without thinking about it. We all love to make decisions with perfectly clear information, but that is not always possible. Sometimes you just have to trust yourself and go with your gut instinct. Why not consciously use your intuition to sense what is really going on with your project?

Celebrate every team member's **birthday.**

Everyone needs to feel part of a group. Why not celebrate all your team members' birthdays and add to the fun on your project? Can you think of fun ways to celebrate a birthday besides just having a cake? How about a game of Pin the Tail on the Donkey (Sponsor), playing musical chairs, or having a fun cake rather than the "normal" kind?

Collect team
members' tales of
adventure.

70

This is what team building is all about. Not only will this be interesting, but it gives each team member a chance to feel special. Everyone has had an adventure, even if it was only in his or her own backyard or imagination. Once you start this, team members will have something to talk about with one another other than just work, and they will feel more like a team. What do you think this will do to their productivity?

Discover whether you've been **micromanaging**

71

What if you weren't at work today, tomorrow, or the next day? Would anything really change? Would it make a difference? Notice what happens if you're not there; you'll discover whether you've been micromanaging. Once a project has been well planned, the team should not really need you. Team members should know what to do and when to do it. Even if a disaster occurs, it's something you should have identified as a potential problem. So why would you be needed every day?

Give **personalized gifts** to everyone on your team.

Do you know your team members well enough to choose something personal for each of them? You should.

Be
invisible...
or not.

Being invisible could refer to not being seen by the sponsor, meaning that the sponsor asks for the project, you disappear, and then you bring him or her a complete project. But not all projects need invisibility. In fact, some projects should be completely visible to everyone. Are you invisible when you should be? Are you visible when you should be? Take a minute to assess how you are working with the sponsor and team.

Publicize
team members'
successes.

The key word is "publicize." Why not let
others, especially a team member's boss, know
when a team member has a personal or a
work success? The workplace can seem full of
negatives, so a positive message will make a big
difference.

Let **go.**

Are you doing everything by yourself? Can you let go and delegate? If not, why not? Do you think no one else knows what to do? If this is your philosophy, you should ask your team members … you might be surprised by their responses. Look at all the reasons that prevent you from letting go and delegating. Are they actually valid reasons?

Have team
member
reunions.

First, ask yourself whether your team members would want to get together after the project ends. If not, perhaps it is time to discover why not, and then make changes on your future projects.

Find something to
admire
about a person
who drives
you crazy.

Everyone has good qualities. If you can focus on the good qualities when dealing with a disagreeable person, you might be able to turn a negative situation around.

A new project manager was given the "worst" team member in the company as part of her team. The project manager discovered that the person had worked there for an extremely long time. The first time the project manager actually met the team member, she said, "I understand that you have been here a long time. I bet you know everyone! Would you mind introducing me to people X and Y? Your introduction would surely help me." In days, that person became the project's best-performing team member.

Have the team
autograph
the project.

78

Let me tell you something that few people know about me: My father helped build the New York World's Fair buildings, which you might have seen in the movie *Men in Black*. As I was growing up, every time we passed the buildings, my father would say with pride, "My name is carved into one of those buildings!" Imagine the increased quality that would result if your team members knew their names would be in the final product. Even information technology projects can have a credits page.

Help others
as if your life
depended on it.

Doesn't it? A person never truly stands alone. Our happiness and business and personal successes often depend on help from others. How can you support those around you?

Make
someone else an
important
person.

Most people want to feel important. Have fun watching the look on a team member's face when you make him or her the star.

Create team
mascots.

Would your team mascot be "The Budget Buster" or "The Charter Chump," or would it be "The WBS Warrior"? Pick a mascot your team members would feel honored to be represented by and watch how productivity and quality improve. How can you have poorly performing project with an inspiring mascot?

Ask a team
member to
teach
you something.

82

Did this one shock you? The real secret is that great project managers can admit to themselves and to others that they do not know everything. Asking your team members to teach you something displays your confidence in them and can help you build better relationships with them.

Chapter 6

Taking
Care
of You

Toot
your own
horn.

Someone has to do it, and you cannot wait for someone else to do it for you. You will get more support for project management if you show how effectively you are using it.

Compare your leadership abilities with those of the historical figure you most **admire.**

Do you admire a political leader, sports star, or a historical figure? Why? You often embody what you admire in others. Why not learn what makes you great?

Protest
a cause.

Stand up for what you feel is right at work or in your community at least once. It will feel so good to speak out. You might even persuade someone to change his or her opinion, and make a difference in the world.

Use your
unused
skills.

Are you a great negotiator who doesn't have a chance to negotiate? Are you a great artist, but have never figured out how to use your artistic skills in the project management field? Are you fascinated by orators, but have never tried public speaking? Is your interest in archeology or history? All of these can be used in project management; can you think of a way? Why not make your days a little more well-rounded by exploring the skills you haven't used in a long time. What unused skills do you have?

Use your
intelligence.

An intelligent person has the capacity to reason, learn, plan, solve problems, think abstractly, and comprehend ideas and language. Are you one of these people?

Get a new
perspective.

Okay, I just wanted to see if you were still reading. And why not read all of these? Hopefully the words will help you in your real world or will at least make you smile. I encourage you to read all of the words in this book, not just the titles.

Speak
in front of
1,000 people.

What could you speak about that so many others would want to hear? Could you deliver such a speech, let alone have something to say? Imagine how good it would feel to be able to help so many people!

Take time to
re-energize.

It could be a vacation or just a quiet lunch at a new restaurant, but everyone needs to re-energize. If you feel tension rising to the breaking point, it is likely that you need multiple recharging moments.

Take all your **vacation** days at once this year.

Imagine how great it would be to leave work for a long time knowing your salary and position were waiting for you. Feel free to go on that long journey.

Find something **positive** in a difficult situation.

A project manager was working on a recovery effort after a major storm damaged an entire region. Instead of focusing on the devastation, the project manager kept a positive attitude by noticing how beautiful the coastline looked. She imagined how lovely the new neighborhood would be when it was rebuilt from scratch. How about you? Can you see something good in everything? Try it for a week. I dare you!

Think like a
5 year old.

Everything is exciting and new to a child. Children can be so easily impressed and amazed. Have you lost those abilities?

Have a permanent
smile.

Why not? After a few years of life experience, you have probably realized that much of what you worried about never happened, and that you just wasted your energy worrying. Realize that you cannot control everyone or everything, and just smile!

Go
parasailing.

Imagine the exhilaration of soaring through the air. Would you feel free? Would you feel like you could do anything? Take those feelings back to your projects, and see how much you can accomplish.

Be a
risk-taker;
go out
on a
limb.

When you are out on a limb, the sun can reach you better, you feel the breeze better, and you can see farther.

Give yourself a
do-over.

Whenever a day just does not go well, call a do-over and repeat the day. See if you can improve on what went wrong. Involving the team can add to the fun when everyone tries to remember what they did the day before.

Explode with
fury
more often.

Is there anything that makes you mad? Of course there is. Why don't you show it? Anger is a way for your emotions to show you the difference between what you want and what is. When you acknowledge your anger, you can look at that difference. If what you want is a reasonable desire, take action to make it happen. If it is an unreasonable one, let go of the anger. Remember, as a project manager you are safeguarding the project's future, your team members' careers, and maybe even your company's future. It is okay to get angry, as long as you consciously acknowledge and manage your anger.

Define **success.**

100

If you died today, what would you want written on your tombstone? How will you measure your business and personal success? If you do not have a measure of success, how can you determine if you have succeeded? Remember, your definition of success will grow and change over time.

Other Best-Selling Titles from RMC Publications

PM Crash Course™ Premier Edition, by Rita Mulcahy
This revolutionary Course in a Book® in real-world project management is perfect for people who are looking to get projects back on track and who want easy-to-use tools that can make an immediate impact. It is also available in audio book and downloadable formats.

Managing the Gray Areas, by Jerry Manas
Managing the Gray Areas explores typical challenges that many leaders of people, projects, and organizations struggle with, and offers a set of guidelines, principles, and tools that can help navigate these murky waters.

Risk Management, Tricks of the Trade® for Project Managers, by Rita Mulcahy

This book offers a proven methodology that prevents many of the problems faced on projects and shows how to manage risks—not simply what to do. This Course in a Book® includes Tricks of the Trade® from more than 140 worldwide contributors, as well as templates, checklists, and practical, real-world examples that you can use to make an immediate impact in your current project.

PMP® Exam Prep, by Rita Mulcahy

This is the best-selling PMP exam prep book in the world. In addition to study material, games, exercises, and Tricks of the Trade®, this book includes enough test questions for nearly two full PMP exams.

PMP Exam Prep System, Fifth Edition,
by Rita Mulcahy

The PMP Exam Prep System includes these three products: a *PMP Exam Prep* book, a copy of PM FASTrack® Exam Simulation Software, and a copy of Hot Topics Flashcards (audio or flip book—your choice). As a system, these products will help you gain the knowledge necessary to get into test-taking mode. These products provide EVERYTHING you need to prepare for the exam

Rita's Pocket PMP® Exam, by Rita Mulcahy

This 3 ½" x 5 ¼" pocket guide contains a complete PMP exam simulation that can go where computers and Internet connections cannot. In addition to 200 of Rita Mulcahy's best PMP exam sample questions, this pocket guide includes an answer key with full explanations for each question and a supplementary index with questions organized by process group.

CAPM® Exam Prep, by Rita Mulcahy
For those preparing for the CAPM exam, this resource includes 12 comprehensive lessons, games, exercises, Tricks of the Trade®, and enough sample questions for nearly one full CAPM exam.

CAPM Exam Prep System, by Rita Mulcahy
The CAPM Exam Prep System contains one of each of three products: a *CAPM Exam Prep* text book, a copy of PM FASTrack Exam Simulation Software for the CAPM exam, and one copy of Hot Topics Flashcards (audio or flip book—your choice).